RUN FOR YOUR LIFE!!

i.am.runner.

Angie Mills

Copyright © 2016 Angie Mills

All rights reserved.

ISBN: 9781729741160

This book is dedicated to my Father:

Thomas M. Mills Sr.

11/06/1949-11/16/2009

He was a loving father, brother, son, uncle, cousin, coworker, friend and one pretty amazing athlete. They used to call him "Tireless Tom" in the hometown newspaper articles. He was a great soccer player, great baseball player and *great runner*. He could hold a sub 7-minute pace for miles and miles. I wish I could say I could do that too.

He is the one who got me hooked on running when I was a child. I have many cherished childhood memories of my father, my brother and I running races together. Our father always ran the longest race and we would run the shorter ones. He pretty much always won first place in his age group. My brother and I sometimes won awards in our age groups too, and my mom has kept newspaper clippings for years of photos of us holding our trophies - the 3 of us lined up, side by side.

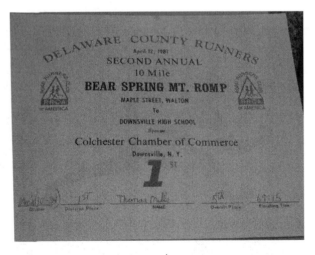

My mom was (and still is) a great supporter of us. I remember her sewing us each our own sweat suit and getting to pick out what colors I wanted. Wow, what a treat that was! My dad always made us wear our sweat suits up until right before the races started and then had us put them back on right after the races. Sometimes that would frustrate me because I have always been OCD about tying my laces exactly right. Then untying them and redoing them. (I am almost 50 years old and I still do that.) And right after I would get them perfect it would be time to take them off to remove my sweats. Oie! He said we needed to keep our muscles warm so they wouldn't cramp up. He was right. We were in Upstate New York and it is cold (or at least chilly) there enough to warrant sweats.

He tried to teach me to pace myself, from a young age, but back then as a young'un I just didn't get it. I wanted to take off like a jackrabbit like so many of the other runners. What? Let other runners get ahead of me?! That was probably frustrating to him. Kind of like trying to teach someone to drive a standard transmission vehicle. But now that I run long distances, I get it, finally!

My dad used to say, "When you are running, think about anything but running, or you'll start to think about being tired and wanting to stop. Keep your mind on something else." He taught us to use our arms when running, and "don't let them cross in front of you" he would say. "Pump your arms" he would say. And he taught us to stretch and move around after a race (or a run) so our muscles wouldn't tighten up. I still follow that advice today. As a know-it-all young adult, at the ripe old age of 23, I made the not-well-thought-through choice to move 2,000 miles away from home, from Upstate NY to Texas, so my dad usually didn't get to attend my races after that time. Although we did talk about all of them afterwards. However, back in April of 2009 he was able to make the trip down to Nashville, TN to see my brother and I run the Country Music Marathon. That was my brother's first marathon and it was my fourth, but it was the first one of mine that my dad got to see. (Sadly, it turned out to be the only one, as well). And it was so great having him there. It was great on all accounts. My sister and her husband were there. My brother's wife was there, and my dad and his girlfriend were there. The weather was *unusually* hot for TN that time of year (near 90 degrees) so it was not ideal for running 26.2 miles, and it turned out to be my second slowest marathon finish time. I had been training in early spring in Texas and the temperatures were more in the area of 50's to 60's. And in TN at that time of year it was expected to be in that same temperature range, maybe slightly lower. Most of the runners had to do more walking than usual because the heat was taking its toll. ***But of all my marathons so far, that was the one I enjoyed the most, because my family was there.*** (Crossing the finish line with no one there to be proud of you can be a pretty empty feeling.) And they were so excited for my brother and I and I knew that to them it didn't matter one bit about how long it took us to finish. We never talked about our 'finishing time'. They were all so proud of us when they saw us crossing the finish line. Their faces just lit up. (Of course, they saw my brother about a half hour before they saw me, lol). And knowing that they didn't care about how fast or slow we ran took all the pressure off me that I tend to naturally put on myself, so much so that I felt proud just to have finished. Afterward I felt great, walking around was easy, I had an unusual amount of energy for having just ran 26.2 miles, I was ready to rock and roll! (I think it helped that I had an "IV Spritzer" right after I crossed the finish line!) Although everyone else in my group was exhausted and sunburned from being out in the heat for hours.

One of the last times I talked to my dad on the phone, (it was on his 60th Birthday) we were talking about running. I would usually call him on Saturday mornings on my way home from Austin, after my long run. I would say something like "I only ran 15 miles today" and he would say "Only?", and in a tone that I knew he meant "Good job!" Sometimes I would joke around and say, "I've been running my ass off, but it doesn't seem to be getting any smaller!" We talked about the marathon I was currently training for (Austin, TX, 2010) and about the new training plan I was using that was different from all the previous ones I've used. I had subscribed to the run less – run faster theory. My running times had been getting faster and I told him that I plan on qualifying for Boston someday, maybe not with this marathon this time, but I was going to someday. And he said "Kid, when you do, that will be one race I won't miss. I don't usually have time off from work that time of year, but I will get the time off and I will be there for that one, definitely." And so, in honor of my father, I will never give up on my quest to qualify for

Boston. Even though he's gone, his spirit lives on in me and through me and I will always work hard to make him proud. And I know that someday, when I qualify for Boston, he will be looking down on me and saying, "Good Job Kid!"

"Wherefore seeing we also are compassed about with so great a cloud of witnesses, let us lay aside every weight, and the sin which doth so easily beset us, and let us run with patience the race that is set before us. Looking unto Jesus the author and finisher of our faith; who for the joy that was set before him endured the cross, despising the shame, and is set down at the right hand of the throne of God." ~ Hebrews 12:1&2

Table of contents

Dedication – To my Father

Acknowledgements

Introduction, Page 2

Ch. 1, Page 7 – About Me

Ch. 2, Page 17 – It's Actually *Not* All About Me

Ch. 3, Page 30 – Who's Idea Was This Anyway?

Ch. 4, Page 38 – Overcoming Obstacles: Everyone Has Them

Ch. 5, Page 46 – Don't Look Back

Ch. 6, Page 52 - My Marathon Memoires

Ch. 7, Page 71 – Benefits or Running

Ch. 8, Page 78 – 'Must-Knows'

Ch. 9, Page 89 – Running Bloopers & Blunders

Words of Inspiration, Page 93

Some Parting Words of Encouragement, Page 94

Book Reviewers, Page 97

Acknowledgements

First and foremost, I would like to give all the glory and thanks to my Heavenly Father, God, for helping me, with no uncertainty, find my passion and helping make it happen. Every run I go on is time well spent in His presence.

I would like to also thank my Earthly Father for teaching me how to run, spawning my love for running and encouraging me in it. I miss our Saturday morning calls on the drive home from my long runs.

My mom who has always been my biggest and most faithful fan. I could finish a race dead last and she would still be cheering for me!

My three daughters, Julia, Chelsea and Isabella, who are such beautiful souls and encourage me to do what I love. Their love for the great outdoors makes my heart sing!

My sister (and best friend for life) for letting me pace her on her very first (and hopefully not last) half-marathon. You'll read about her inspirational story later in this book.

Samantha Scarborough for the awesome book cover art!

My brother for also being a runner, a big-brother/protector guy, a smack-talking smartass and for being someone I can talk to about running. We give each other the push we sometimes need to get moving!

My track coach in High School, Coach Hoover at Walton

Central School, for putting up with my not-always-great and sometimes sassy attitude and being a great encourager anyway. He helped make running fun. I'm not saying getting the dry heaves under the bleachers after sprint repeats was fun. But if you've ever been on a high school track team, you'll know what I'm talking about.

My marathon training coach, Paul Carmona, for teaching me so much about endurance training and how to properly train for and successfully run 26.2 miles – and still want to keep doing it again and again!

The 'guy on the plane' that suggested I write a book about running. Our brief conversation was enough to confirm for me that I should just do it! Sometimes God sends us Angels in disguise, appearing as normal, real people, to send us a message from Him. I can't say for sure, but I think this may have been one of those times.

Introduction

We have all heard about how there are many health and wellness benefits to running:

- It reduces your risk of heart disease
- Improves the function of your immune system
- Reduces/relieves stress
- Helps with weight loss/maintenance
- Relieves pain from tension headaches
- Reduces risk of developing high blood pressure and can help lower High blood pressure
- Improves cardiovascular and respiratory systems
- Reduces risk of developing Type II diabetes
- Lowers resting heart rate
- Can help improve bone density
- Can help regulate the mood swings of menopause
- Strengthens muscles
- Runners report mental clarity, keeps your mind sharp
- Helps you age gracefully
- Helps you maintain a healthier emotional attitude
- Runners are less angry, fatigued and depressed than non-runners
- Can help improve short term memory
- Reduces medical and healthcare expenses
- And on and on… so much more!

The benefits of being a runner are great, no doubt, but for me, it's not about the benefits listed above, so much.

Running defines me. It's who I am. It's what I do. It's what I love. It's my passion. It's about carrying on the family tradition. It 'runs' much deeper for me than just the health benefits. I don't have to prove myself to anyone else. I can't recall ever feeling like I needed to prove anything to anyone. Other than myself. Running a marathon (or even a half marathon) is about setting a high goal and proving to *Myself* that I can do it. That I can commit to something, I can set my mind to it, I can stick with it even in the hard times, despite any and all obstacles in my way and accomplish it. My dad said to me once, before my first marathon, that "to want to run a marathon is a lofty goal". He was a great runner. And even to him it seemed like a huge goal. He understood what that would take. And he was right. Twenty-Six Point Two miles is huge. You don't just wake up in the morning, put on your running shoes and head out the door for that many miles. It takes a lot of training, learning, planning, rehearsing, dedication and motivation among other things. Having a supportive family (or friends) would be a big benefit as well. But it can be done. And if you prepare for it properly, it can be the most awesome experience of your *athletic life* - crossing that finish line is an amazing feeling of accomplishment! (As much as I Love Running, I won't put that alone on a pedestal as the 'most awesome experience' in life.) It is something truly unforgettable and irreplaceable. And the finisher's medals are pretty cool looking.

Although I reference the full marathon and half marathon distances the most often in this book, I want you to know that I believe *any race distance* you do is worthy of praise!

You don't have to run a full marathon, 26.2 miles, to be awesome! When you make up your mind to do any race, and you train for it and are dedicated and committed to doing it (be that running or even a run/walk combo, or just walking), and you get out there and do it – **You Are Awesome!**

Every runner has their own story - some funny, some awful, some embarrassing, some heart-warming, some great learning and some hugely inspiring. Within the pages of this book I plan to share with you my life, as it pertains to running. I will share with you the humorous side of running – as seen through my eyes – the ups and downs we all face, the regrets, the learning, the joys, as well as the pride that comes with accomplishment. As I mentioned before, I love running, it's my passion and it is my hope that this book about running brings you smiles, smirks, laughter, giggles and Teehee's, an occasional tear of joy and that it inspires you to carry on with your running (or whatever it is you do that you love!) I also hope that as you are reading this book, you learn a little something about running, that you'll find some inspiration and motivation to get you moving and that you are hearing the song "Eye of The Tiger" in the background playing over and over!

"But it is good to be zealously affected always in a good thing" Galatians 4:18A KJV

It's good to be passionate about certain things, just make sure they are good things, as in not sinful or against what God instructs.

We all go through some down times – times when our enthusiasm, motivation and/or dedication feels like it took a hike and left us standing at the trail head – and in times like that it can help to read about other people's experiences to get us jump started again. As I am sitting here typing this, looking out my window at all the birds desperately pecking through the thawing slush to find food, I am daydreaming of when the temperature gets back above freezing and the roads aren't coated in ice – so that I myself can get back out there and go for a much-needed run! It is also my hope that you will search within yourself and find what it is about running that you love, why you do it, (or think you would like to start), what keeps you going, why you refuse to give it up. Because I don't believe it should be just about the "benefits" you reap, but more rather about something inside you, deep down, about You believing in Yourself, about doing what you love and not something you do because you think you should. About proving to yourself that you can. Proving to yourself that you can start something great and stick with it. About battling those voices inside your head that are saying, "just stay home with a cozy blanket on your lap and watch some TV". ***After all, running isn't always easy. But it's always worth it!***

If you ever need some words of encouragement, email me or call me. I'm here for you. Maybe running just isn't your thing, but I encourage you to find what is and tackle it head on!

You can do it – I believe in you!! You are strong! You are determined! You are courageous!

> *"I can do all things through Christ who strengthens me!"*   *Philippians 4:13*

Chapter 1:

about me

When my dad got done tying my sneakers for me, (he always tied them a little on the snug side) we went to the school and ran laps around the sports fields, in the very small town of Downsville, NY. I remember having fun being outside, in the fresh air, but getting a little worried about having to go potty and not seeing a bathroom anywhere! I can also remember my dad lacing up my ice skates on me and making sure they were nice and snug around the ankles. Can't remember how young I was, but I must have been young enough that he needed to tie my shoes for me.

Fast forward to Junior High School: my friend Kristie and I made the High School soccer team (the only 2 players who were in 7th grade and on the Varsity team) and my dad showed up to referee one of our home games after school. I guess I didn't realize, until then, that he was a soccer referee in his spare time. It would make perfect sense, though, since he was a hometown superstar soccer player growing up.

My dad never bragged about how good he was. Therefore, as a child, I never even realized just how good of a runner he was. It wasn't until I was an adult, had completed several marathons of my own, and was sorting through my dad's things after he passed away. I came across his finishers certificate from that 10-mile race in Downsville that showed his average pace of 6 minutes and 56 seconds per mile. Wow! I wish I could run like that!

I have been running since I was a child, as far back as I can remember, but according to my mom (my biggest fan) I started running in actual organized races when I was about 7. My father was an amazing athlete. He was great at any sport he did - baseball, soccer, running. But

> Success is no accident.
> It is hard work, perseverance, learning, studying, sacrifice and MOST of all,
> *love of what you are doing.*
> -Pele

running was his main event and he could keep a sub 7-minute pace on a long run. I don't expect to attain to that kind of 'athletic prowess', but I did inherit his determination and dedication. He required it of us to participate in sports as we were growing up. There was no laziness allowed. No staying inside on a beautiful day! He didn't impose just one sport upon us, but rather gave us a well-rounded taste of many sports/activities (except for basket weaving! I chose that on my own in elementary school.) We did a little bit of everything, played soccer and softball/baseball, swam, ran, ice skated outdoors for hours at a time whenever the ponds froze over, used our sleds as snow-boards before snowboarding was a thing, hiked, roller skated, chased foul balls at his baseball games, anything and everything. But running is the one thing I've always stuck with. Maybe because you can do it anytime, anywhere, all year, in a gym, on a treadmill, on a trail or a well paved road…

I have the sweetest memory of this one particular race my younger brother and I ran, back in 1981. While our dad was running his 69-minute 10-mile race, we ran the shorter 2-mile race. I was 11 and my brother was 9. This was a small race, in a small town in Upstate NY (Downsville, to be exact) so there weren't a whole lot of participants. I remember shortly after we got started my brother got scared of being alone (acceptable reaction at the age of 9 on a desolate county road) so I let him catch up to me and I held his hand literally the whole way out and back. At that time, I was probably feeling more irritated and put out by it, but looking back, I love it that I did that. I'm sure to him it probably felt like I was dragging him along, but I don't remember him complaining about it. I must have ditched him the last few yards though, because my finisher's certificate shows my time being 6 seconds faster than his. Sorry little brother – I love ya but that competitive spirit was already in me!

As an early teen, and pre-teen, I remember getting up on weekends and going out by myself, right after sunrise, and going jogging or just walking out on worn paths, in nature, enjoying the peacefulness. Sometimes it would be foggy at first and I would get to watch the fog burn off.

Occasionally I would have a chance sighting of a bunny rabbit or other small animals. Little did I know there were black bears and bobcats in the area. It's probably good that I didn't – I may not have gone out alone. I just didn't have any fear. Back then.

I remember one time when I was about 13 or 14 and I went out for a run with my dad. I thought we'd run about 2 or 3 miles, the usual, but little did I know he was taking me on a 6-mile run. To me, back then, that was a lot. I remember being so dog tired and he just kept telling me I could do it, keep going, breathe, and so on. It must have been torture for him to run slow enough for me to keep up. Or maybe that was his idea of spending quality time with his daughter? Either way, for most of the 6 miles I thought for sure I was going to drop dead. Totally, completely, dead. But it sure felt good when we made it back home and I could say I did it. *(I didn't have to follow up my "I did it" with "but it almost killed me". Some details don't matter.)*

In high school, I ran track every year and loved it. It helps that I was a decently fast sprinter. I usually did the short and sweet races. Run like crazy for a few seconds and you're done! I tried cross country one season, but I didn't do very well. They ran more miles than I imagined I could, at the time, and I was never fast at long distance. Mostly, looking back, I think it was just a lack of self-discipline. Plus, I was the only girl on the team that year, and I just could not keep up with the teenage boys.

As an adult, I have participated in more 5K's, 10K's, triathlons and Half Marathons than I can remember. I can, however, remember all of my Marathons. Each one has taken on its own personality, with its own story of ups and downs, and when you're out there for 3 or 4 hours (or more, sometimes) a lot of memorable things happen!

For my first Half Marathon I was training with a fitness trainer from Gold's Gym and she wasn't really a runner, so I didn't learn a lot from her, but I managed to finish the run and I still craved more. The thing I remember the most about her was that she just kept complaining about the smells of other runners. Someone must have put on a spritz of perfume before the race, God forbid, and it just drove this girl crazy. Oh yes, and I remember when we were driving to the race, she had us going the wrong way on a One-Way street!

Austin, Texas is a mecca for fitness enthusiasts, whether your love is running, yoga, hiking, or whatever else. There is no lack of fitness opportunities there. I heard about this brand-new marathon training group for women, called Twenty-Six Point Two. It was a free training program; you just had to qualify and apply and get accepted. To qualify you had to have completed at least one Half Marathon, which I had by the time I was applying. I was accepted into the training group. This was the Inaugural Group. We trained together, 3 times per week, for about 4 months before our marathon – the San Diego Rock 'N Roll Marathon. This was such a great opportunity for me because as a single mom (of 3 daughters) I couldn't have afforded to pay for this coaching program. Had it not been for the great coaching provided, along with all the comradery and sisterhood, I don't think I could have completed 26.2 miles. And even though I was in a lot of pain when I finished that first marathon, I was hooked! I couldn't wait to do it again! I just knew I did need to allow myself to heal from this one first. (If you would have seen me walking through the airport the next day, to catch my flight back to Texas, you might have thought I looked like I got run over by a bus!)

At the time of the start of this book, I had a running/walking group that I coached in Austin, TX. I love coaching and getting other people on the same band wagon. I have previously been a Certified Fitness Instructor and Specialist in Performance Nutrition, as well as Certified Marathon Trainer. My business DBA was SIU Fitness – standing for 'Suck It Up'. That is something my oldest daughter (in HS at the time) used to say, a lot. It seemed applicable. I do a lot of studying up on fitness and nutrition and I love sharing that information with the people I coach, to help them make their own improvements and hopefully get as hooked on fitness as I am. People are always saying "Do what you love", well…this is what I love!

I wasn't gifted to be a super-fast runner, but I was given

the gift of Determination. Grit. Perseverance. Sometimes

to a point beyond stupid! I have said many times that I don't quit something I start, and if I ever don't finish a marathon (or any other race) it's because I died. Done. Kapoot. I'm just that way. Competing not against the other people around me, but against myself, my own strength, my own determination, my own will. Fighting the part of me that feels like a lazy sloth. Not allowing myself to get talked out of reaching my goals, by myself or anyone else. Not allowing myself to take the easy way out. Pushing myself so that at the end of the day, I feel good about the person I see when I look in the mirror.

In high school, one time (my Senior year) I was feeling back stabbed by my teammates on the field hockey team and told my mom I wanted to quit the team. She was adamantly against that. One of the things she said was "Winners Never Quit and Quitters Never Win". I quit the team anyway, out of foolish pride. (Oh boy was she ever mad at me!) And I regretted it for a long time. I think that negative experience has contributed a lot to me being so determined to never quit again something I start.

I ran a 10K race once, in Albany, NY, with a stomach ulcer. I found out that my extreme stomach pain while running was an ulcer about 2 weeks before the race. I had been training for a while by that time, I had already signed up, paid the registration fees, my mom had a T-shirt made for me... there was no way I wasn't going to do it. During the race, it was so painful that I had to actually just stop a couple of times (OK, a few times more than a couple). But I crossed the finish line. Last place, literally (119 out of 119). Dead Last! But I still finished. Quitting was not an option. It may have been in the past, the far back past. But it's not an option anymore!

As far back as I can remember, I have always enjoyed writing. I have written many poems, some of which have been published and one which I was asked to read at my High School Graduation Ceremony. (I would love to have a copy of that now.) I've written outdoor adventure articles for a magazine in Austin, TX (once about rock climbing, once about zip lining, just to name a couple) and I've written articles on LinkedIn related to business (mainly Human Resources) topics. When I was a teenager my mom gave me a hardcover, fabric covered book with blank pages, for me to fill in. Inside the front cover, she wrote "My dearest Angela, this book is for all the wit and wisdom inside of you!" I wish I still had that book.

But one thing I have always loved the most is running, and I've always wanted to write a real book. That makes this seem like a great match up!

You know how sometimes you meet someone, even if for a very brief time, (maybe even just minutes or hours) and they leave such an impression on you that it stays with you forever (it seems)? Well, here is one of those times in my life.... On a flight back from Nashville to Austin, traveling home from the marathon I just ran there, I was chatting with the gentleman sitting next to me. As it turns out, he was an author, and had several books published already. We talked about the reasons we were each traveling that day. For me it was traveling home after the marathon in Nashville, TN. He told me he was an author and I expressed my love of writing and how cool I thought it was that he was an author. After chatting for a while, he ever so nonchalantly said "Why don't you write a book about running?" He reignited the spark on the inside, for me! The rest is history. He didn't even know that had always been a 'secret' dream of mine. To be able to combine my love for running with writing is like pairing the best wine with the best cheese!

Chapter 2:

it's actually *Not* all about me

As I have mentioned before, I have always loved running and been running since I was 7 years old. But as I've gotten older, I've learned to accept that it's not all about me. There is so much satisfaction in helping others learn to run, to coach them and help them train for an event, to water the seed of love in a runner at any level, and to help them reach their goals.

Jackie's story, which you'll read next, (it's very inspirational so get a box of tissues ready – for real) is just one story of a runner stepping outside of their own little world and into the world of someone else and helping them reach a goal. Jackie's goal was to run a Half Marathon in honor of her (our) father, as he was a lifelong runner and huge inspiration to us all – and had just passed away a few months earlier. She was never really a runner before this. In high school she was more of a girly girl on the cheerleading and gymnastics teams. As opposed to my kind of sport, like being the goalie on the girl's field hockey team and running track. So, this was a pretty monumental goal for her.

I enjoyed coaching her in her several months of training and, I won't lie, I enjoyed pacing her about as much as I have enjoyed completing any other race I've done for myself. Here is her story….

In Honor of Our Father:

By Jackie Mills Van Loan.

It all started after our Dad passed away (November 2009). He was a runner; my sister and brother were also. Me, not so much.

Dad came to Tennessee in April 2009 to watch and cheer on my sister and brother as they ran the Country Music Marathon 2009, in Nashville.

In January 2010, 2 months after Dad passed away, we all decided to train for the Marathon and Half Marathon in April. My sister would pace me for the Half Marathon and our brother would run the full Marathon.

I had run a couple of 5K's prior to this but I knew the Half Marathon would be my most difficult, but the Best!

I really didn't take time off; I wanted to be ready because I would have to keep up with my sister…. And we all know she is competitive!

I felt good running. It cleared my head and kept me healthy. I had every muscle in my body screaming and would have cramps, even my fingers and toes would hurt. But this was for Dad.

In January I began "my journey". I began by walking every day, diet changed and had my music to keep me going.

By February I was running a mile a day and progressed to 3 miles, then 5. It was tough but I kept hearing Dad say, "go on, you can, just another mile". He didn't push us but rather encouraged us in all aspects of our lives.

We had all decided to have special shirts made for our race. It really wasn't a race for me. I just wanted to finish.

We all got to Nashville, the night before. We all had a great dinner, then off to bed. We woke up and got ready for a long day. We were excited and sad at the same time. We arrived at the race site and there were so many people, everywhere. I was so nervous and had to go to the rest room. We hugged, and fist bumped, and went over and got in line. I was shaking. We got set and the gun went off to start – and off we went!

My sister set our pace, knowing I wouldn't be able to run as fast, but stayed by my side. We walked then ran, walked then ran.... I saw the 5-mile point and was like, "Crap, 8 more miles... but I can do this!"

We had a pee break, and water of course. It really was amazing. We were in stride. She kept saying "You can do it! You've got this!" There were runners that cheered us on and said, "For Your Dad!!" There was music and spectators cheering as we ran by.

I was a beautiful day! Well, up until we got to the last mile or so and the sky opened up and started raining. We rounded a bend and I saw "FINISH".

I was crying, and my sister and I crossed the finish line holding hands and so thankful we made it!

We Finished!! And we had a finish time of 3 hours and 28 minutes. That was better than I ever expected. Well, I expected to finish last, but we didn't and oh what a feeling it was to finish!

We looked for our brother to watch him cross the finish line and he did amazing also! It was a great experience and one check off the bucket list. I won't do a Half Marathon again, but the memory will last my lifetime.

I love my sister and brother for getting it done and "This Run's for You, Dad!"

> *"At mile 24 in the Chicago Marathon, it hit me that I was definitely going to make my best marathon PR! I scrambled to find the song "Party Rock Anthem" by LMFAO and listened to it on repeat while waving to the crowd all the way to the finish line. It's the little things that give you the motivation to finish strong and smile big!"* ~ Eva Oleksy

After my first experience pacing another runner, I really had a much greater appreciation for all the pacers I've ever seen at races. They could be out there running for themselves, but they are out there helping other runners.

It's pretty amazing!

I have a friend, named Amy, who also started running shortly after we met, and early on asked me to help train her, her having not ever been much of a runner previously. When she first started running with me, we did a lot of walking, and that's OK. Gradually we did more running than walking. I coached her along and taught her as much as I knew, and she got to the point of being able to run a good enough distance that she wanted to run a Women's Half Marathon and asked me to be her pacer. We signed up for a race in Bastrop, Texas that was women only (mostly… there were a handful of men that didn't take the hint at the name of the race "Women's Half Marathon").

I remember throughout the race that as Amy was getting tired, she was getting irritable, but not in a serious way. (Although it's probably a good thing she wasn't carrying any sharp objects with her!) I think she sputtered a few cuss words in my direction, but that didn't stop me from being my jovial, perky self! I was just dancing along, bouncing up the hills, encouraging her and cheering her on, as well as the rest of the sisterhood out there around us. I was cheering on everyone. Giving out 'high 5's" to keep those women motivated and excited! I had such a great time doing it. I had no pressure on myself as far as a finishing time, or to finish in a top certain percentage, so I just got to have fun doing what I love – encouraging other people and building them up! Being a cheerleader, so to speak.

Amy may have been irritated with me during the race, but I know after she crossed the finish line of her first Half

Marathon, she appreciated my over-enthusiasm. And the joy I felt, as a pacer, from seeing someone else reach their goal and feel so proud of their accomplishment, it's indescribable. It made getting up at 4:00am worth it!

> *I didn't think I had a moment to share, especially about my first marathon, but when I thought about it today, I did have a moment during my last marathon. I ran the REVEL Mt. Lemmon Marathon on November 12, 2017. It was the first marathon that I completed in under 4 hours and my first ever Boston qualifying race. At about mile 21 I realized that if I could hang on I had a real chance to qualify for Boston. It was a feeling I had never experienced before, and one that I didn't really believe I ever would experience. It made me realize that I had a lot more mental toughness in me than I thought. I finished the race in 3:56:21, with a Boston-qualifying cushion of 3:39. I am currently training for the REVEL Mt. Charleston Marathon on April 28, 2018. My plan is to try to add another minute or so to my cushion. We'll see if that happens! ~ Katie Carmona*

Being in the Austin, TX area, which is a mecca for fitness, many volunteer opportunities present themselves. Some of the most memorable ones for me were:

Volunteering at the finish line of the Austin Marathon. Our running coach, Paul Carmona, was on the race organizers committee and he had asked if any of us would be interested in volunteering for the marathon. I have volunteered for this race twice, during years when I wasn't running in it. The first time I was the finish line water tent coordinator. I had lots of other volunteers helping in that area/tent throughout the day. My daughter and her friend came with me, even though it meant they had to get up at like 5 am with me, to get there in time. It was more fun than it was work. We just handed out bottles of water to the runners as they walked by.

The best part of volunteering at the finish line was getting to see all the half marathon and marathon finishers right after they crossed the finish line. Seeing the different reactions among them. Some were all excited, jumping up and down cheering, some were crying tears of joy (maybe tears of pain) as they hugged their loved ones who greeted them there. Every journey, every race, every finish is special. It was an honor to get to be a part of that.

The other time I volunteered at the finish line of this particular race was as a finisher's T-shirt tent coordinator. Again, this was more fun that work. It was so enjoyable congratulating everyone that came through, who had just finished the race. And seeing everyone celebrate their accomplishment.

I remember this one woman in particular who crossed the finish line just before the 'sag-wagon' was collecting runners off the race course. There is always a cut-off time to finish by so that the roads on the race course can be reopened to traffic. Anyway, this woman did not look like what you might imagine, as far as someone who would run a 26.2 mile race. She was very heavy, I'm guessing around 300+ lbs. It was super exciting, and inspirational, seeing her cross the finish line because she was proof that you don't have to be a skinny little bitty to run that far. You just have to want to do it and be willing to work for it. And at the end of the day, she ran just as many miles as all the runners – including the ones who finished in 2 hours! So there, anyone can run and finish a race!

One side bar I must note is that all area coordinators (which I was both times) were given really spiffy running jackets (with the Austin Marathon logo on them) and running sneakers. From what I understood, this was in part a way of keeping us all color coordinated and easily identifiable, but it was also a really cool thank you gift for volunteering our time. I'm not saying you should volunteer for what you get out of it, though. The joy you feel on the inside, for helping others, in any capacity really, is one of the best reasons to volunteer. Running races aren't the only events that need volunteers. I was blessed with the joy of being a "Swim Angel" for 2 of the Danskin Women's Triathlons in Austin. And one of those triathlons I volunteered on the racecourse, directing cyclists. The first time was 2 or 3 weeks after my first full marathon. That probably wasn't the best timing, because I was still recovering from my race. But it was very therapeutic for me. Swimming is a great recovery activity for sore muscles, and helping other women get through the swim phase was healing to my soul as well. The 3 specific women I ended pairing up with, on my first time as a swim angel, were all seemingly scared of the water and that half mile swim appeared to seem insurmountable to them. I don't think they realized what they were in for before that moment. So being able to swim beside them (I had a floatie I gave them for their sense of security) and talk them through it and encourage them was so rewarding for me – and I'm sure they really appreciated it. Sidebar: I didn't swim the half mile with all 3 women at the same time, it was 3 different trips for me. The swim angels would swim around the half mile area, get out and go back to the start and find another woman that needed assistance. So, each one got some one on one assistance.

As I mentioned previously, I have coached a running group in Austin (a small group of runners from my church and some of their friends), and, also for a season I coached running for a triathlon club I was a member of in Kyle, TX. But when you volunteer your time, it doesn't necessarily have to be in something that you are a super star in. There are opportunities all around you if you look for them. I've coached many seasons of youth soccer, while my 3 daughters were all playing (over the course of about 7-8 years). I've been a volunteer mentor at one of the elementary schools my daughters attended. We've done clothing drives for flood victims. I've volunteered on my cities Parks and Rec Dept. Organized a race as a fundraiser for an injured police officer. Served on my HOA as President for a term. Volunteered as Secretary in 2 of my Neighborhood Watch programs. So I encourage you, if you haven't already, to step outside of your own little world and volunteer some of your precious time in areas where it's needed. Two things I haven't done yet, that are on my 'bucket list' – volunteer at the building of a Habit-For-Humanity house and go on a Christian mission trip.

> *"But they that wait upon the Lord shall renew their strength; they shall mount up with wings as eagles; they shall run, and not be weary; and they shall walk, and not faint."* ~ Isaiah 40:31

Not all of my family were necessarily into sports or athletic. (Mind you, I come from a large family! My paternal grandparents had 13 children – a baker's dozen - and my maternal grandparents had 10 children. And they have all been fruitful and multiplied. So, I have even more cousins than aunts and uncles.) But I do know of a few that were athletic. As I've mentioned before, my father. But also, a couple of aunts and uncles, and some female cousins. My Uncle Bill was telling me once about how he just went out for a run one day and ran 20 miles. As in, he didn't carbo load and hydrate properly the day before. He didn't have water stops along the way. He didn't make sure he was wearing the right running shoes. No Body-Glide. Didn't take any gels with him. Kind of like Forest Gump when he went out for a run one day and just kept running.... And ran across the whole United States. Gimme some of that energy! One of my cousins has run a handful of marathons, (so a pretty healthy and fit person) and believe it or not, she survived a heart attack in her mid-thirties. One of my other female cousins, who is a few years older than I am, was an athlete as well.

Here is her story:

"I was an athletic kid in school. Loved playing every sport. Recently I found all my old trophies while cleaning out my mom & dad's house. I was pretty good! L.O.L. I even got outstanding Senior Athlete! As I reminisced about my years in school I thought how I never really liked running. I never did track but I loved shooting a soccer ball at the goal, or making a basket from the free throw line, and I was a pretty darn good pitcher in softball. I just remember never really liking running. Strange how the tables turn.

A few years ago, I joined a fitness studio in my home town. I loved working out. Then I found out that the woman who owned the studio was organizing a 5K run in my home town!!! That was pretty exciting to me and at the age of 46 I signed up!! I did a program called Couch to 5K. It WORKS! 8 weeks of training, you run a little, walk a little. Each week you increase the amount of time you run. By the end of the 8 weeks you should be able to run, without stopping, for 25-30 minutes, which is the approximate time it takes to complete a 5K. My girlfriend and I trained together and finished that race together in 32.7 minutes. Not too bad for our first run. Afterward we looked at each other and said "what do we do now? We can't just stop, we've worked hard to get where we are." So, you know what we did? In my best Forrest Gump impression, we were RUNNNNINGGGG!!! Never stopped, we have completed several 5K's, 10K's, ½ Marathons and I have a full marathon under my belt. I have some health issues, I honor my body but at the age of 52 I am still running, and I have come to LOVE it!!! Who'd a thunk it. Where the mind goes, the body will follow."   Dawn D'Addezio

Chapter 3: whose idea was this anyway?

Do you remember when you first started entertaining the thought of running a race, a 5K, a 10K, a Turkey Trot, a Jingle Bell 5K, a triathlon, or even a marathon? Do you remember where that thought originated from? Why did you want to do it? What is your motivation? What draws you to it? Is it your passion? Did your doctor tell you to start doing it? Were one of your parents (or both) a runner? Did you get started in gym class in school?

> *"I've run 3 marathons now, each one I was at a different phase in my life, each run I was battling a different war...but each victory at that finish line tasted the exact same."* ~ Jennifer Riojas-Santos, First timer with Twenty-Six Two 2014

Here's part of my story: I was married at one time, and we had 3 beautiful daughters together. (Now it seems like a lifetime ago.) But, like too many of us, unfortunately, we ran into some serious relationship problems. And neither of us knew how to handle it, I didn't know how to help him, and he didn't know how to help me. Needless to say, we were not very good communicators. We were stupid and selfish and didn't know what to do. One of the problems was, as with many couples, your world eventually starts to revolve around your children and you stop putting the effort into your relationship that is required, if you want it to last. And who doesn't. I mean, I think we all get married with full intentions of "until death do us part", not divorce. Sadly, we eventually separated, and later got divorced. Looking back now, we can see how selfish and self-centered we were (or I least I see it clearly, now) and realize we should have put forth more effort. The saying is true, "Hind sight's 20/20". ***Our relationships with the people we love are so much more important than anything else in our lives. Yes, even more important than running.*** Please always keep that in mind. During this very difficult time in my life, after separating from my spouse, I started spending time running with my friend Raquel. Her husband would babysit my girls while we went for our runs. We would meet 3 times a week after I got home from work, and he would watch the girls while we ran. My daughters were like grandchildren to them, so it worked out great for all of us.

> ***Our relationships with the people we love are so much more important than anything else in our lives. Yes, even more important than running.***

And as all runners know, that run with partners, or running buddies, we tend to talk about our lives. Sometimes, perhaps, we divulge too much information. Sometimes, maybe it's like free therapy to have someone to talk to about it. Maybe that's just us women. Racqui and I would talk about the problems I was going through and she was always very supportive. The one thing I think I wished she would have done was straight up tell me to get my act together and work out my relationship problems with my spouse. Her and her husband had been married for over 30 years at that time, and no doubt, had to deal with some tough stuff too, throughout all those years. I still cherish her friendship, absolutely, because she was always a listening ear, she loved me and my daughters unconditionally, she taught me some unseemly phrases in Spanish, (such as 'besa mi fundio') and she got me started on the road to running longer distances. With her I started running 6 miles, which for me was a good distance at that time. She ran it every day, so it was no big deal to her. Eventually we were running 8 miles each outing and it seemed to come so easy. We never pushed ourselves to run fast, we just really enjoyed the time that we were out there running. It really was a great form of therapy.

For me this was a stress reliever and I would look forward to the mental break and to doing something that was for me. That is something we often lose when we get married and become parents – doing something that is for ourselves and not for our spouse or children. For a good 10+ years my whole world revolved around others and now, *as my world was falling apart*, I found reprieve in this thing I was doing for myself. Maybe it was a little selfish, but maybe it kept me going in such a difficult time in my life. Maybe it kept me from falling into too deep of a depression. Yes, I'm sure it did. I had, during this dark time, lost nearly 25 pounds and for someone my size, that was like 20% of my body weight. Too much. (Don't worry about me though – I have 'found' all the weight I 'lost').

I'm not sure when I first heard of running marathons, or where they were or anything about them at all really. I didn't even really know how far a full marathon was, at first. I had always done a lot of 5K's and 10K's, but nothing more. Yet. I do recall a conversation with some friends of mine, they were not big-time runners or anything, and we were talking about marathons and how many miles they are, and I was commenting on how crazy that was. So many miles. How could anyone do that? Wow! Amazing! And my one friend said, "Well, you don't have to *Run* non-stop the whole way, they aren't going to chase you or make you run without stopping. Some people walk a little too." When she said that, a light came on in my brain! I didn't mention to anyone right away about how much the thought of running a marathon seemed appealing to me. I didn't want to set a gigantic expectation for myself, before I was sure I could succeed at it. I for sure didn't want to make a fool of myself by talking about doing something, and then not being able to do it.

I have been a runner for over 40 years now, (not saying I'm a fast runner and I haven't qualified for Boston, *yet*, I'm just a happy-to-be-running runner at this point), but it wasn't until I was in my mid-thirties that I hopped on the marathon wagon.

One reason it drew me in was that I like doing things that

are hard, really hard, a challenge, unimaginable to some, things that *not everyone* can do (athletic things anyway). Something that some might call a lofty goal. And when I exercise, I like to be thoroughly exhausted when I'm done, else I feel like I didn't work hard enough. I was also motivated by the fact that few people believed in me when I first said I was going to run a marathon – then the race was on! No pun intended. It became a matter of proving to myself that I could do it. Maybe it was more than that too, maybe it was a matter of life and health for me. As I mentioned before, I know it helped me fight off serious depression. And after the first marathon finish line, I became addicted. Some people, after their first one, realizing it is a little punch-drunk crazy to try to run 26.2 miles ~ in one day, decide right then never to do it again. For me, crossing the finish line was so amazing that I couldn't wait to do it again! I may have failed at one of the most important relationships we have in this life, but I felt like I succeeded at this.

> *"Running a marathon brings out the best in you. It makes you dig deep and find the grit you never knew you had inside of you. Training for a marathon with a group of women you never met makes you realize that when we work together for a common goal we are better as a team."* ~ Amy Cobb

I remember when I was training for my first marathon…. At that time, I used to go to a local Baptist church's women's group one evening per week. This was something recommended by my Pastor at that time, who I counseled with as I was dealing with my marital problems. I remember having a conversation there once, with the church ladies, talking about all the obstacles that kept coming up trying to interfere with me doing that marathon. Some of the ladies said, "Maybe God is trying to tell you not to do the marathon." I said "Huh, the way I see it is He is the one who has helped me *overcome every single obstacle* so far... so it must be OK with Him." They all had blank looks on their faces :) I wasn't trying to be a smarty pants, but I do believe some dreams/goals God puts in our hearts and He is going to help us succeed. God does not put obstacles in your way to try to get you to give up.

Running has been much more to me than just exercise. And I have, at several times in my life, had people make me feel guilty for wanting to spend a half hour or hour on myself, for myself, to go for a run. Like I was being selfish. If I had a quarter for every time I heard "All you care about is yourself" or "what about making dinner?" and that sort of thing, I would be a rich woman. Even with all the running I ever did, I still managed to take care of all my responsibilities. Wow! It's not like I was going to the strip club or spending the rent money on fancy golf clubs. I was running, God Sakes. Something we all know is good for us. (Unless for some health reason your doctor has advised against it.)

> *After finishing his first marathon, Tommy says to Kathy "If I ever start talking about running another marathon, hit me in the shins with a baseball bat!!"*

I have recently been reading "The Purpose Driven Life" by Pastor Rick Warren. In Day 9, he makes reference to the movie *Chariots of Fire*. That stuck out to me. I can relate to the runner, Eric Liddell. Here is the paragraph in the book I'm reading:

> In the film *Chariots of Fire*, Olympic runner Eric Liddell says, "I believe God made me for a purpose, but he also made me fast, and when I run, I feel God's pleasure." Later he says, "To give up running would be to hold him in contempt." There are no unspiritual abilities, just misused ones. Stare using yours for God's pleasure.

I am by no means fast, and certainly nothing like Eric Liddell. But the passion he feels for running, I feel it too. And I'm not sure when it started, as in when I got hooked on it. But I definitely believe it is a passion God put in my heart. And I feel like for me to give up running, I'm giving up something God gave me. So, I don't. I can't. And it isn't always easy – running. I have my obstacles. I just choose not to use them as an excuse.

> *I believe that we can walk through any valley we're facing and stay focused on getting to the other side. I believe that for me God has always held my hand... (He is my 'Footprints in the Sand') and whenever I have stumbled or fallen, He has helped me get back up again. I haven't finished any race or any challenge or any life difficulty without Him. As it says in* **Philippians 4:13 "I can do all things through Christ who strengthens me."**

Chapter 4:

overcoming obstacles: everybody has them

When I would hear about runners that complete marathons and half marathons, before I ever did, I used to think (maybe not consciously, but just sort of had the impression) that they all must be in perfect health and everything in their life must just be rosy and perfect, making it possible for them to do what they do. It definitely never crossed my mind that they may have struggles they have to deal with – obstacles they have to overcome. Little did I know.

I've never heard Anyone *ever* say, "I've never had any obstacles to overcome in my life, ever."

Once I started running more, and training with a group, and meeting other runners and getting to know more about them, it became clear that Every Runner has some (maybe many) obstacle they must overcome, some struggle, some challenge they are dealing with that others may know nothing about.

One of the ladies I met in a marathon training group was dealing with a failing marriage at the time. She had been quite overweight but had successfully lost over 80 pounds, and that seemed to be causing marital problems.

Her husband wasn't as excited about her weight loss as she was. Why, you may ask? Maybe because her self-esteem and confidence had improved. She was more attractive. She felt really good about herself. Perhaps, instead of rejoicing with his wife for her great accomplishment, he started feeling insecure? Whatever the actual reasons were, I know it was a very difficult time for her. Not only was running doing her health a world of good, but I believe it was also a very healing opportunity for her emotionally, as well.

I met an older woman, years ago, in Austin, we'll just call her Wonder Woman. She seemed to always be at all the local 5K and 10K races I was at. She always stood out in the crowd, mainly because she always had on cheetah print clothes, always smiling and she was in her 80's! I have always loved spending time with older and wiser people than myself, so eventually I went to her and introduced myself. As time passed, and we became friends, I learned a lot about her. She didn't even start running until she was in her 60's. That was after she nursed her husband and mother (at different times) until they passed away. Then when she had time for herself, she took to running. She did vastly more than just the local 5K and 10K races, she did track meets, and even endurance races much further than marathon distance. She even made it into Runner's World Magazine at one time. They did a one page write up about her, her story, and all of her accomplishments. What an inspiration that woman was to me! And to so many others too, I'm sure. She had private struggles she was dealing with in her life, but she didn't let that stop her from doing what she loved!

There have been many times, through the years, that I wished I could run just a little faster, just a little farther. I was always decently fast, but never quite the fastest. When I would run in 5K's, 10K's, triathlons, and so on – I consistently finished in the top 20%, but never won my age group. The older I got, the more self-discipline I developed, and I was able to run farther. However, shortly after I was realizing that I could run a long way, for a long time, I was also discovering that I had some health issues. After I had already completed my first marathon, and several half marathons, I started noticing some problems that were developing and seemed to be causing some trouble.

I remember after one of the half marathons I completed, I had an unusually difficult recovery. At the time I didn't think much of it, other than thinking I was probably just a little more dehydrated than normal. Then shortly after that, I had gone to my local YMCA and did one of the pretty aggressive Les Mills workouts (which normally wouldn't have been a big deal for me) and the next few days I was so sore and having so much pain and stiffness, I knew something wasn't right. I had been lifting weights since high school, and in college even gave body building a try, so I knew how my body should feel after a tough workout. This was worse.

I can't recall which marathon it was that I was training for, but I started noticing, after my runs, that I would have unusual pain and stiffness, especially in my hips. It didn't bother me while I was running, but after runs, and after sitting for a while, when I would get up, I could hardly move – it took a minute to loosen up. Finally, I went to see my doctor, who referred me to a sports medicine clinic. They did a bunch of tests and didn't find a good explanation. They did see some bone spurs in both hips, which would cause some pain, but that didn't explain the pain and stiffness everywhere else. They mainly just chalked it up to overtraining (as I was spending about 14 hours per week, either running, biking, swimming, or working out at the gym). They gave me a prescription for some special elixir mixer cream to rub on my hips where the pain was, and I used that until after that particular marathon. It seemed to give a small amount of relief.

As time passed, I just kept noticing more issues, and made a few more trips to my doctor. Finally, he ran every test he could think of, and found what might be a problem. He did a test called ANA, anti-nuclear antibodies, and my numbers were through the roof. That tests for systemic autoimmune disorders. So, my doctor referred me to a Rheumatologist. The first one I went to treated me like a nut case. She thought it was all in my head. I could tell by her tone of voice, the way she rolled her eyes, and said I just needed to take sleeping pills. I changed doctors. The next Rheumatologist was great. He was a marathon runner too, so he understood me! He did more tests of his own and determined that I have RA (Rheumatoid Arthritis). On the one hand, it was a relief to know what was going wrong and causing me so much trouble. But on the other hand, it was not great. Running is one of the worst things (if not the #1 worst) you can do when you have RA. It's hard on your body. The good news is, there are medications you can take, and dietary changes you can make, that help.

In the past 8 years or so, since I found out about having RA, I have used several different medications. Most of them worked pretty well for a while, then they would lose their effectiveness, so we had to move on to the next one. The one that probably helped my symptoms the most, but I also hated the most, was one where I had to give myself an injection once a week. I used to be terrified of needles, but after all I had gone through on the road to finding answers about my health, needles had become just another thing. I had gotten used to them. I just hated taking that medication because I knew I was injecting a poison into my body, to fight another 'poison', so to speak. Eventually, mentally, I couldn't stand taking it anymore, so after about a year of it, I stopped.

I have tried different dietary changes, some of which help tremendously – like sticking to a Gluten Free diet – and some haven't made much difference. I have tried several natural remedies, such as ground flax and cinnamon (which I put in almost everything I bake), and turmeric (which I put in all the meats I cook). I think the best thing I've tried (and still use today) is Turmeric Curcumin and Black Pepper in tablet form.

Anyway, the point of sharing with you (an abbreviated version of) my journey to finding out about having RA, is to share with you that through all that, I did not give up running. This is a huge, ongoing obstacle, one that I have to overcome daily. I have pain and stiffness every day, regardless of what medications I take, what diet I follow, what supplements I use (they all help some), but I still just can't fathom the thought of giving up running. It's breath to me.

One of the wisest pieces of advice my Rheumatologist gave me, right off the bat, was that I needed to learn my new limitations. He said he wasn't going to tell me to stop running, because as a runner himself, he understood how I felt. But I would need to listen to my body more and temporarily pull back sometimes as needed.

Looking back, I would say that RA was affecting me long before I was diagnosed with it. I probably could have run faster, and maybe even a little farther (more comfortably) without it. But I will never use it as an excuse to become lazy and sedentary. I can't do that – it's not in me. I just may end up running a little slower than I prefer.

What obstacles or struggles you are facing today? Or have faced in the past? Or have you had some that you have risen above, conquered, or defeated already? Obstacles and/or struggles don't discriminate. They present themselves in everyone's life, at some time or another. Sometimes the obstacles or struggles we face are put there by our adversary, the devil. The first step to overcoming them is recognizing this fact. When the devil (who does exist whether we think so or not), tries to stop you or interfere in your life (and he will), you need to stand up to him, get in his 'face', and tell him to go back to h-e-double hockey sticks where he came from.

These can be physical struggles, like health issues, of which there are too many to name. They may be short term or ongoing difficulties. Or they can be mental struggles, such as depression. Emotional struggles like going through a divorce or mourning the loss of a loved one. Obstacles can be things like lack of time to exercise, because you are a single parent and your children need all your free time. A lack of funds to buy the gear you need or pay race registration fees.

One thing I know for certain, is that where there is a will, there is a way. Sometimes we may have to modify or adjust the way we do things, or the frequency or intensity with which we do them, but we can still find a way to do the things we love.

> 1 Peter 5:8 "Be sober, be vigilant; because your adversary the devil, as a roaring lion, walketh about, seeking whom he may devour:" ~ God

Chapter 5:
don't look back

One of my aunts once told me, before one of my high school track meets, "Remember Angel Face, don't look back!"

Looking back can mess up your stride, it can cause you to trip and fall, give the racers behind you a chance to catch you, mess with your head, and it can surely slow you down from reaching your goal. I recall a 400-meter relay once, where I looked back for just a split second too long after receiving the baton, and I tripped over my own feet and wiped out! On my face! Wow – talk about embarrassing! It's awkward and embarrassing enough sometimes just being a teenager, but then add wiping out during a relay race at a track meet with grandstands full of spectators to that. Some things scar us for life. I literally kept finding scrapes on my body for a week after that. And apparently, I am pretty emotionally scarred, since I still see it clearly in my memory, after all these years.

In the same way, in 'life', looking back can be bad for you. I am, of course, referring to looking back on the past. The skeletons in the closet past. (I mean, if you hear a huge animal chasing you when you are out jogging alone down a country road, looking back might be a good idea – to assess the situation… and get out the pepper spray or run faster!) Looking back at good times, sweet memories can be fun, even be a blessing. That's OK, of course. But when we start looking back on the bad things, the negative things, the things we regret, the things we wish had not happened, or happened differently, things we wish we could change…that can impede us from moving forward. Don't let what's in your past hold you back from what's in your future.

Have you ever done something you regret? Said something that afterwards you wished you could take back? Whether that was while drinking alcohol or not? (The raw truth is that what is in your heart comes out your mouth. Alcohol just makes it come out easier sometimes. So, don't try to say you didn't mean what you said, it was just because you had too much to drink!) Have you ever reacted to something in a way that made a fool of you or hurt or embarrassed someone else? Have you ever done something that you have a really hard time forgiving yourself for?

Of course, you have. We all have. (I realize my name comes from the root word 'Angel' but I also realize that I have not always been 'angel like'). There are seemingly little things we do that we feel bad about afterwards, like flipping off the crazy driver on the highway that cut in front of you and almost hit you (then you realize it's someone from your church). Or saying a cuss word at a totally inappropriate time. Or drinking too much and trying to sing karaoke at a child's birthday party. And then there are those big mistakes that we painstakingly regret like being unfaithful to a spouse or significant other. Or getting involved with someone else's spouse or significant other. Or looking at something online that we know we shouldn't. If you are being totally honest with yourself, you know you have things in your past that you did wrong, things you are not proud of. You know that if you are being honest, you will admit there are things you regret, things you said that you wish you could take back. Times that you reacted, instead of acted. Times when you walked away and shouldn't have. Times you should have walked away and didn't. Maybe a time when you should have been bold and stood up for what you knew was right, but you let your fear cripple you? Or maybe something worse. And if you don't regret or feel bad about any of the awful things you've done, I would suggest you get professional help. Seriously.

I hate to be the bearer of bad news, but you can't take it back. None of it. You can't undo the past. You can't claim a mulligan, (life isn't a golf game), no do-overs. You can't take back the ugly things you said. The hurtful things you did. You can't undo the streaking naked down main street after the party. You can't unbreak your wedding vows. You can't unhurt your child's feelings after yelling at them for spilling their drink on the floor. You can't take back all of your jack ass remarks. I think this life would be a lot easier if we could. No, I *know* this life would be a lot easier if we could. And I love to be the bearer of good news! We may not get Do-Overs, but we do get Second Chances! You can ask God to forgive you for your sins, (and various other misdeeds), first and most importantly. And wherever, and whenever, possible, you can apologize and ask for forgiveness from the person you hurt or offended. (If you haven't already read the 12 steps from Alcoholics Anonymous, I highly recommend it, whether you have a problem with alcohol or not. It's good advice for everyone.) Sometimes it's not in someone's best interest for you to go back to them to make amends, just to ease your conscience. Use your head on those issues. You can still ask God for forgiveness. And you can, and need to, forgive yourself. You can change your actions. You can change the way you respond to situations. You can learn to bite your tongue and think before you speak. Get that filter installed in your mouth if you need to! You can learn which things in life are more important than others, such as being faithful to Your spouse is more important than having some pretty woman flattering you and trying to lure you away from the woman you *actually* love, to build up her own sick ego. (Obviously, the reverse is true here too). Refer to my previous comments about Relationships with the People in your life being the most important thing. Don't be a Narcissist. I hope you'll pardon me for being so blunt, but some things in life just need to be said, and I've pretty much always been the one to stand up and speak. That's what true friends do. They tell you the truth, even if they know it's not what you want to hear. I know I don't want someone being a 'yes man' to me, I want my friends to be honest with me – even if what they have to say my hurt my feelings or make me feel like poo for being a jerk. Sometimes we need someone to slap us up-side the head and help us get back on track! None of us need to be told how terrible we are or how bad what we've done is. We already know that. But sometimes we do need someone to point us in the right direction. Tell us what's up. And we can – and should - learn from our mistakes and be smart enough NOT to repeat them. Stop hurting the people you love!

Don't be a jerk to people just because you can! If you are miserable, and that's why you are a meanie, go see a therapist and figure out *why* and how to change. There are plenty of self-help books for us to read. One really good one a friend shared with me is called "Feelings Buried Alive Never Die" by Karol K. Truman. It has changed my life.

God knows us, He made us, so He knows we will screw up. So, He may have started with Plan A for our lives, but then He has Plan B, Plan C, Plan Z, whatever it takes. Don't keep messing up just because you know you will be forgiven. But know that if & when you mess up, you can ask for forgiveness and receive it. And from then, try staying on the right track. Every day be working on being a better person than you were the day before. And like Cousin Paul always says, "There's the original plan, there's the modified plan, and then there's what actually happens."

And running, in many ways and for many reasons, can and does make people happier. So, keep running. Keep trying to be the best you possible, in all areas of your life. And stop looking back.

Chapter 6:
my marathon memoires

My first marathon was in San Diego, CA with a group of first-time marathoning women. The training group/organization is called Twenty-Six Two. (They are still around and going strong today!) I trained with this group in Austin, TX under the coaching of Paul Carmona. He was (and still is) a very helpful, encouraging and knowledgeable & experienced runner and coach (who had completed over 60 marathons so far). I learned a lot training with him.

I had no idea, when I first started training for a marathon how much there is to know about Endurance Running.

We learned about:

> - The importance of hill workouts, speed workouts, tempo runs and long runs.

> - We learned about preparing for our runs, days in advance, and the proper way to carbo-load and hydrate.

> - We learned about different carbs and the importance of where they fall on the glycemic index.

- We learned about using gels/goo's on long runs. And to follow them with water and NOT a sports drink!

- I discovered that drinking out of a garden hose won't actually kill you. And that if you are thirsty enough, it may taste delicious!

- We learned about how to prepare the day before a long run (simulating marathon race day) so that every time we hydrated and carbo-loaded properly and trained our bodily 'systems' to always 'empty out' first thing the morning of long run, before the run…. therefore, eliminating any need to stop on the run to use the restroom.

- We learned that your body can only absorb about 8 oz. of liquid every 15 minutes or so. That way your body can use the liquid more efficiently (for hydration) and not just pee it out. (And avoid having to go pee on a long run).

- I learned, from our speed workouts on the track, that I have 'exercise induced asthma' but that using an inhaler pre-workout can prevent problems during a workout.

- I learned how painful post-run sports massage is! (I guess sports massages aren't necessarily supposed to feel good, they are supposed to speed up the healing process.)

> I learned that I was good at pacing myself and that I could run faster and longer than I ever thought possible.

~~~

So here is what I recall from **my first 26.2-mile race**. It was in San Diego in June of 2006. I trained with and traveled with a group of first-time marathon women, Twenty-Six Two, from Austin, TX.

We flew in on Friday afternoon, got settled in. Saturday, we went to the race expo and did some wandering around and exploring, then later did a little 2-mile easy run together and some stretching together and mostly rested. We also took a tour of the race course, (via bus) but it's not like I expected to remember it while I was out there running it. What I do remember from the tour was a black Dodge Magnum car that I thought looked cool, and it seemed to be driving the race course too because it was right there most of the tour.

Race day, I was up by 5am. Partly because I couldn't sleep, I was too excited and way too nervous! I like to get up early anyway, so I have time to hydrate a bit, eat a little something (usually a piece of toast) and have time to go poo poo. You never want to have to stop during a race to use a porta potty. We headed to the race, quite prepared and a little early. I never like to get to a race just in time for the start. As it is, I always have a bad case of the butterflies, so if I were having to rush, that would make it even worse. Our group all met up and wished each other well and all that fluffy nice stuff.

We got lined up in our corrals based on our expected finishing time, bounced around a little to warm our muscles up, enjoyed the upbeat and cheery music and announcer, listened as each corral ahead of us took off, and then, off we went. We were all in different starting corrals based on our ability, and not necessarily with anyone from our group. I was in corral 4.

Everything seemed to be going great for a while. I was paying attention to keeping my own warm up pace, taking my gels on time, grabbing water and/or Gatorade as planned. I printed off one of those paper pace-bracelets you laminate and wear or take with you, to help you stay on your pace, mile after mile. I did really well with it, up until about mile 15 or 16 or so. I enjoyed all the spectators along the course cheering us on, giving words of encouragement. Someone was yelling "Relax your shoulders!!", which helped me notice I was tensing them up – so I relaxed them. The little children cheering was (and still is) my favorite! Eventually, all the highway on-ramps and angled roadways we had to run on, started taking their toll on me. I had been struggling with IT band problems at the beginning of our 4 months of training, but with a lot of pampering it had stopped being a problem, until about mile 18. The pain gradually kept getting worse until it reached the point that I could no longer fully bend my right leg with each step. For those of you who have ever had IT band problems, you know what I'm talking about. Nothing helps other than to stop running when it's hurting – and that was NOT an option for me. Not even a consideration. I did, however, get so overcome with pain, around mile 23 or so, that it started to drip out of my eyeball sockets in the form of water or some other sort of liquid…. Thank God I had sunglasses on, so no one could see! It wasn't pretty. But I just kept plugging along. Plugging, limping, by that point it was all the same…. My waterproof mascara held up quite nicely, I have to say.

About a half mile before the finish line you could see, from a good way off, a huge archway. I thought that was the finish line, so I cheerfully increased my pace slightly, thinking I was almost done. But as I got closer to the arch I realized it was just that, an arch, an advertisement for a particular brand of running shoe – whose name I won't mention, because I was not pleased with them at that time. The actual finish line was still about another half mile away. Ugh! On the one hand, it's like, "Whatever, I just ran nearly 26 miles, what's another half mile?" but on the other hand it was like "Oh my gosh, are you kidding me right now?!?" Finally, as I neared the Real finish line, I thought I heard someone calling my name! First marathon. First time running 26+ miles. A little delirious. Turns out it was my running coach, Paul C., and he was at the finish line handing out finisher medals to runners right after they crossed the finish line. I headed over to him, he gave me my medal and a hug. In that 10 second hug, I broke down crying like a baby. I couldn't hold it in anymore. He may have thought I was crying tears of joy, which is a pretty normal reaction for a lot of first-time marathon finishers (after all, it's a pretty overwhelming and unforgettable experience), but the reality is that it was tears of severe pain. And maybe some tears of joy too, in knowing I finished, and the most painful part was over! Thank you, Jesus!

> *"There is no way to recapture the feeling of your first marathon finish. Whether you are a one-and-done marathoner, or run 100 more marathons, remember that feeling of your first finish line."* ~ Paul Carmona

After the finish line, we had a meeting area where our group was going to all meet up and catch up on how everyone did and pass around 'congratulations!'. I remember they gave us some green crocs, meant to be comfortable, and a silver foil 'blanket' to help us warm up if we needed it. My favorite was the teensy-weensy plastic cup of beer every finisher got after the race. We worked hard for that 4-oz. of beer and it tasted so refreshing! Even though my leg was still killing me, I was just so happy and relieved that the hardest part was over. It's kind of like that feeling of relief after giving birth. You don't feel great right away, but you feel relieved that the most painful part is done.

Before we left Austin for this marathon, we had all pre-scheduled massages with our massage therapist, who traveled with us to San Diego. I remember when it was my turn for my massage, post-race, I was so stiff and looking forward to my massage. But oh boy, that was so painful. I think I had that weird thing happen again where some strange liquid was leaking out of my eyeball sockets. Sports massages aren't exactly relaxing like a Swedish massage, but they are so good for you, working out knots and toxins and all that bad stuff, and they speed up your recovery. It is kind of a paradox, inflicting pain to aid in healing/recovery.

I remember walking through the airport the next day, for our flight home, and I literally could hardly walk. I wore my finishers medal, like a badge of honor, on the outside of my jacket in case anyone wondered why I was walking so funny. But I can tell you without a doubt that the amazing feeling of having finished my first marathon totally overshadowed the pain I was still in. And I knew for sure that I was going to do more marathons! *I loved the fact that it was so ridiculously hard, and I did it anyway! I proved to myself that I could persevere and do something that I set my mind to, no matter how hard it got.*

Pain is Temporary, Pride is Eternal!!

Marathon number 2 was the Austin marathon, in February of 2007, called the AT&T Austin Marathon at that time. The Austin marathon is in mid-February each year, right around Valentine's Day. (All the Texas marathons are during the winter months due to the heat in the summer. San Antonio is November, Dallas is December, Houston is January and Austin is February.)

Anyway, this day was very cold by Texas standards, with the start of the marathon being 28 degrees. By the time I finished it was only 32 degrees. The electronics at the starting line were malfunctioning due to the freezing temperatures. And rather than serving donuts at the finish line, they shifted gears and had hot chili in bowls ready for us. Along with hot chocolate! This was of course in addition to the usual finish line refreshments.

I typically run better (by better, I mean faster) in colder weather, but I don't necessarily prefer 28 degrees – 40's would be perfect! We knew before race day that it was expected to be unseasonably cold. As we were waiting for the race to start, huddling out of the breeze wherever we could to stay warm, they announced that the race start time had to be moved back one hour later because they were having to go along the race course and spread salt to de-ice the slick areas on the roads and bridges. I don't recall anyone jumping for joy at that announcement, but you just know, after months of training in various weather conditions, that anything can happen on race day, so you should be mentally prepared. I was. That was my best marathon finish time so far, so I can't say the weather was a bad thing in my case.

An important thing my running coach taught me was to set progressive goals, not one set in stone goal, for each marathon. My first marathon, in San Diego, I finished about 30 minutes slower than my goal time (due in great part to the IT band problems that came up), but I still had a great finishing time, (for me) especially for a first timer. I was beating myself up about it and my coach finally talked me into getting that monkey off my back. So now I set progressive goals and I met 3 of my 4 goals in my second marathon. We'll talk more about goal setting later.

Before this marathon, my running mate Katie had offered to pace me for the last 6 miles of the race. When I got to that point and she saw me, she jumped onto the race course and ran the rest of the way with me. She was awesome! Believe it or not, my fastest miles out of all 26, were the last 6 which she ran with me. She cheered me on, cheered me up, made me laugh, even got the crowd cheering for me. She was a chatter box (which was great) and at one point, I was working it so hard and she just kindly let me know I didn't need to talk too. If it weren't for her, I probably would have only reached 2 of my 4 goals that day. That was the first time I had someone pace me for a race and I have since enjoyed pacing a few people myself – and I got to see just how rewarding that can be!

The only disappointment of that day, (and trust me, I don't want to point fingers or place blame), was that someone was supposed to bring my daughters to the race, so they could see me cross the finish line, but that person decided it was too cold outside and didn't want to bring them. The whole marathon I kept thinking about seeing my daughters at the finish line, cheering me on and how excited they would be to see me, and how excited I was to have them greet me. That thought helped me keep going and keep my chin up during the toughest parts of the race. As I was crossing the finish and had crossed it, I kept looking around for them, but eventually realized they weren't there. So, I pouted all the way back to my vehicle, walking on my sore, frozen feet. I did later find out that they were as disappointed as I was. They made signs and hung them on the front door for me so when I got home I would see them. Now that they are adults and can drive themselves, I do hope that someday they will be able to be at the finish line waiting for me!

> *Too often we make the mistake of remembering what we should forget - our hurts, failures and disappointments - and we forget what we should remember - our victories, accomplishments and the times we have made it through.*
> *~ Joel Osteen*

Marathon number 3 was in San Antonio, TX in November 2007. This was a Rock 'N Roll marathon, so of course they always have good music and entertainment and a great race course, as far as the volunteers and water stops and first aid stations, etc. I have to say though, there are two things I would change about this race course: there is one section you run through that has a nice archway of trees shading the road, but the problem (in the race I ran there) was that there were a lot of holes in the road that you couldn't really see if you were wearing sunglasses – due to the way the sunlight was streaming through the trees. It was beautifully majestic, but I would maybe consider diverting through an area that was easier to see, even with shades on. The other thing I would change is how the finish line was at the top of a hill. We had to run up hill for about the last quarter mile or so to get to the finish line. Not preferable, after having run 26 miles. Sometimes that last quarter of a mile feels easy, but sometimes it seems to go on forever.

Here's what I remember: the temperature at the start of the race was in the mid 30's (around 37 to be exact) and by the time I finished it was in the 60's. Normally that would be fine. The problem that it gave me was that my feet 'shrunk' a little in the cold (at the beginning) and swelled a little after enough miles (which is expected), so by the last 1/3 of the race or so, I had giant blisters covering the whole bottoms of both feet – from my feet sliding around in my shoes.

While I was running through that shady area mentioned above, I stepped in one of those holes in the road that I didn't see and twisted my knee. It hurt pretty bad, to the point that I had to sit for a minute. And after I started running again, I had to stop and walk a few times because it hurt so bad. After that point, I knew it wasn't going to be one of my best finish times, so I decided to drop the pressure of that and just enjoy the rest of the race. I took every opportunity to run over to the sidelines and high five all the little kids that were holding their hands out. And I eventually took my knit gloves off, as it was getting warmer, and gave them to a little girl who was there cheering on the side of the road. I chatted with a lady running next to me, who had been keeping pace with me for quite some time.

I didn't have that monkey on my back anymore, so I really soaked it all in. I even grabbed a small solo cup of beer from one of the spectator tables that was set up along the race course. Refreshing! I figured since I wasn't worried about my finish time anymore, I may as well have fun!

After the race, I stopped at a medical tent and got ice

packs for my knees and headed to my car. I have to admit, it felt kind of gross walking on squishy feet, but I sure was glad to elevate them after I got home!

Marathon number 4 was in Nashville, TN in April 2009. This is the one that my brother ran also, and our Dad was there for. I remember my father joking about my running capris. He called them knickers. He said when he was looking for me to cross the finish line, he was just going to be looking for my green knickers. Yes, he was a pretty funny guy!

For this marathon, I had been coaching my brother long distance during the training phase. This was his first full marathon. We talked on the phone several times per week, as he was in TN and I was in TX. He has a lot of natural athletic talent, so I had complete confidence in his ability.

Race morning, we got to the race later than planned, due to traffic jammed up getting to the race course. Cutting it so close on the arrival time causes me a lot of anxiety. I'm the type of person that likes to get there an hour ahead of starting time. I like to use the port-a-potty 5 times before the race, wander around a little, and tie and re-tie my running shoes 12 times before the race begins. I didn't get to do any of that this time. Once we got parked, we headed toward the starting line. I didn't eat anything at my brother's house before we left and had planned on grabbing a bagel when we got to the race. We were too late for that. I think all we had time for was to use the porta-potty (just once), drop off our race bags and get in line.

My brother ran with me for a good warm up distance, but eventually he had to go do his own thing. He is way faster than me and I wanted him to see how good he could do and not be held back by me. The fact that he is about 7 or 8 inches taller than me, which means longer legs, longer strides, probably helps in the faster thing too… hahaha.

The weather in Nashville at that time of year is typically in the 50's to 60's. As we know, weather can be unpredictable, and this day was no different. We did know a couple of days in advance that it was going to be unseasonably warm, but our bodies weren't prepared for the heat wave. It was in the 70's and sunny first thing in the morning and warmed up into the low 90's. I give the race coordinators a big pat on the back because when they found out about the heat wave, the did beef up on water stops, ambulances along the course, first aid stations and they even had volunteers literally handing out salt packets on the race course. You know those little salt packets you get at fast food restaurants. They did everything they could to make it a safe experience.

Mentally, pre-race, I had decided that it was not probably going to be optimal to run my fastest marathon ever, (due to the heat wave) so I shifted my thinking and decided to just ENJOY IT. Again. And that I did. Best part – high fiving all the kids on the side of the road who were out there cheering us on! This is one of my favorite marathons for many reasons. One of them is that they have great entertainment all along the race course – makes sense being in Nashville and all. Country Music Capital of the World. Anyway, it was ridiculously hot and sunny, and I eventually had to give in and walk a little. Most of the runners were walking too, so I didn't beat myself up about it too bad. I remember reaching the top of a hill, and as I was starting on the downside and had a great view of the course ahead, I could see literally hundreds, maybe a few thousand, runners all walking. So I didn't look at my walking as a failure – which is something that in the past I would have thought. Later in the race I remember jogging alongside this female runner and asking her if she knew how much further until we got to the 25-mile marker. It seemed like it was taking forever. Mind you, I was reaching pretty serious dehydration by that point, (on top of not having eaten anything for breakfast and going on a few gel packets) so I wasn't thinking all that clearly. I was thinking we were around or just past the 24-mile mark. So, she tells me, "We passed the 25-mile marker a while back… we are almost done!". I was extremely happy to hear that! As a matter of fact, I think I shed a few tears of joy. And right after I crossed the finish line, my sister greeted me, and I agreed to go to the medical tent for IV fluid treatment. This is the marathon I mentioned earlier in this book where my family was in attendance. And were all super proud of my brother and I.   Best. Marathon.   Ever.

Here's what I recall about **Marathon number 5**. This was Austin again. February 14, 2010. This time it was different. A lot of things had changed in my life since the last time I ran the Austin marathon. This year it was actually on *Valentine's Day*. The race organizers had asked for runners to write in about their 'story', why they love to run, why they are running this marathon, etc. and the race directors were going to choose 3 stories to publish in their magazine that goes out in all the runners race packets at the race expo.

My dad had just passed away 3 months before this marathon, and understand, even though I am a light-hearted, happy-go-lucky, joke-around type, just as much as for anyone, this was extremely traumatic for me. The day my brother called me to tell me that our dad just passed away, my world came crashing down. Nothing else in the world mattered to me at that moment. At first, I thought my brother was playing some kind of joke on me. Sick joke. I didn't believe him. I said, several times, "Tommy, this isn't funny, don't joke about this shit!" It took him a few heart wrenching minutes to get through to me. When I realized he was being completely serious, I just hung up the phone with him and started screaming "NO!!!" and crying harder than I ever thought a human could. How could this happen? He was one of the people I loved the most in the world. I was not ready for this! Tell me I was dreaming. Say it wasn't so. *I was on a plane back to NY later that night.*

I decided to submit my 'story' to the marathon committee, although I didn't tell them what I just told you, but see below – it's a clipping of what I did write in. They chose my story as one of the 3 for their magazine, out from among something like 3,000 sent in. That was a bitter-sweet honor, to say the least.

Run for Your Life!!   i. am. runner.

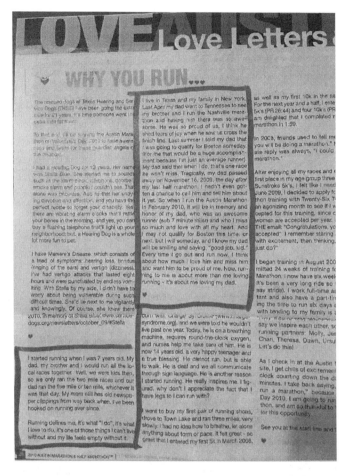

I had done all the training and preparation for this marathon, like I knew I should. But some situations are beyond our control. I had developed a kidney infection in the week before the race. I had noticed, while I was at my desk at work, that I wasn't feeling well. I paid a visit to my doctor and she did some tests and called back and let me know about the infection. I explained that I had a marathon in 3 days and needed to get well. She says to me

"I'm not going to be able to talk you out of running this weekend, am I?" She knew the answer to that. So, she gave me a prescription for an antibiotic to start taking right away and told me to protect my skin extra from the sun, as I would be more prone to sunburn while on that medication. She also encouraged me to stay hydrated, and she wished me well.

That last couple of days that I had to get ready, I just couldn't eat. I was feeling so sick from the infection. No carbo loading. I didn't hydrate properly either. Everything upset my stomach and wanted to come back out. Not at all ideal.

Race day came, and I was as prepared as I could be, all things considered. I knew going in that I would not DNF, (unless I died on the race course) it just may be a tough race. My friend, Gary, who was in the running group I coached at that time, was running the Half Marathon that day and he ran with me until our race courses split – about mile 9 or 10. While I was running with him I was fine. I think having someone to talk to helped keep my mind off how I was feeling. However, shortly thereafter, I started feeling quite ill and couldn't ignore it. I made my way over to the side of the road a few times, feeling like I was going to vomit. Although, there wouldn't be much to vomit. Dry heaves, I suppose. I hadn't been able to take my gels because I was feeling so sick to my stomach. I was barely even able to sip any Gatorade or water at the water stops.

Although I was quite sick, before-during-and after this race, I kept a pretty positive attitude. I can remember as each mile ticked away, I was doing the math and telling myself how few miles I had left to go. I do this sort of tallying in my head, to keep my mind occupied, where, each time I pass a mile marker, I say how many miles I've done and how many I have left. At mile 20 I remember thinking, "I just ran 20 miles, I *only* have 6 more miles to go. Awesome!". Yes, I seriously did think that. I wasn't looking at it, like some people might, like "OMG, I *still* have 6 more miles?!" When I finished, I remember feeling pretty good about my attitude, especially considering how challenging of a day it was. But in my heart, I was doing this race to honor my father. And since my story was picked as one of the 3 Love Letters for the marathon magazine, giving up was not an option! It never is in my mind anyway. It never will be. And I did finish! My finishing time doesn't matter, so I didn't beat myself up about it. It was not as fast as I would like. But, it usually never is. And that wasn't the point anyway. Finishing, and not quitting, was the point.

Chapter 7:
benefits of running

In the first chapter I noted a few benefits to running. Here I would like to talk a little more about some of those. Some of my favorites.

My Disclaimer: Understand, I am not a licensed medical professional, I am just sharing what I've learned and experienced in my 40+ years of running. You should always check with your medical care personnel before trying anything new.

Weight management. You can use running to help you lose weight, but you'll need to combine that with other factors besides just running. You need to eat a healthy, well rounded diet, and for some people that may mean a big change. That's OK. There are plenty of resources to help you get started on the road to eating better. Over the years I have tried several different dietary 'theories' that I've read about, to test them out. I've never had to deal with losing *a lot* of weight, but I have on occasion worked to lose a good 25 pounds. Everyone is different, so what works for someone else may not work for you. And likewise, what didn't work for someone else, may work for you. One of the things I've always suggested to people (who were soliciting advice) is to keep a food/drink journal. Write down everything you eat and drink in a day and keep track of the calories of each item. This benefits you in several ways; sometimes it can be a major eye opener and let you see that you don't hydrate enough, or you drink too many soda's, or you eat way more junk food than you thought. And a million other possibilities. And you can take that information and analyze it to see what changes you need to make or could make. And if you are one of the rarities who are trying to gain weight, maybe it will help you see where you can make changes to help you gain the (healthy) weight you need.

It's a Feel-Good Drug. A legal one, and guilt free too! A healthy Anti-Depressant. A great mind/body connection. It causes a release of endorphins which can cause a feeling of euphoria (think, happy). Running is actually used quite often to treat depression. It can reduce tension, depression and confusion.

Some ways it can help reduce stress is by allowing you time, (the time you are out running/jogging) to think about any problems or cares and spend time thinking about solutions. You might be thinking about these things consciously or in the background. You can listen to music and meditate – which gives your mind a break from what it is 'worrying' about. Many solutions to problems have been found out on the hike and bike trail. You can incorporate hard workouts (like hill work or speed work) to help burn off some frustration or negative energy.

It's better than Botox. Running, on a regular basis, can help keep you looking younger than any pill or injection you can buy. As I've mentioned before, I've been running my whole life, basically (since I was 7) and I have always received comments about how I look much younger than I am. When I was 23, pregnant with my first daughter, I was mistaken for a 16-year-old unmarried teen. (Pretty sure that woman felt silly after her comments). One time I was picking up one of my daughters from middle school and the attendance clerk asked if I was her sister! Nice! And more recently, I had someone comment on how she could not believe I had a 25-year-old daughter. I do attribute this a lot to having been athletic my whole life, but I'm sure good genes and great facial moisturizer have contributed.

Running can also keep you 'younger' in terms of energy levels. Just getting up and moving your body, stretching your muscles and strengthening them, lubricating your joints, hydrating well, being outdoors and allowing your body to produce Vitamin D ~ it's all a great cocktail for boosting your energy!

It's good for your heart. Running can lower your risk of heart disease by large percentages. What percentage is going to depend on how much you run, how consistently and how long you've been running, coupled with your overall other health. Distance running also has the added benefit of stronger heart-parts. They generally have lower resting heart rates and have higher maximal oxygen consumption, so they can take in more oxygen while exercising – which fuels their running (or other activities). Running combined with strength training can produce even better heart results. Running, jogging and brisk walking all can produce similar heart health benefits.

> *Beans, Beans, they're good for your heart. The more you eat, the more you fart. The more you fart, the better you feel. So, eat your beans with every meal. ~ author unknown*

I will mention that I do believe it's possible that too much running can potentially be bad, and what is too much for each person is going to be very subjective. And it may not be the running, per se, that is the culprit. It can be overuse (running too much or too hard, more than your body can handle), poor running form (causing knee, ankle or hip injuries), not getting proper rest and nutrition, bad running surfaces or bad running shoes, to name a few. Knowing your body and having a doctor you visit regularly will help you determine if you are running past the benefits and into the 'red zone'. There have been some studies that suggest that excessive running, over a long period of time (years) which would be most common in marathoners or ultra-marathoners, can cause a thickening of the heart valves, as well as potentially causing the arteries and chambers to stiffen up. More reason to stay in touch with your physician.

> "Holding forth the word of life; that I may rejoice in the day of Christ, that I have not run in vain, neither labored in vain." ~ Philippians 2:16

It boosts your energy level. Better than a cup of Joe or any energy drink! Yes, that sounds crazy, you would be inclined to think exercising tires you out, but it actually energizes you. There have been many studies of participants suffering from various issues or illnesses that can cause fatigue, and they all point to the fact that regular exercise increases your energy level. I know this, as well, from my own experience. I have RA (Rheumatoid Arthritis) as well as Fibromyalgia, so I have many times when I feel very fatigued, and I have found that, even if I don't think I can manage to run that day, if I just at least get out and walk, I feel better. It energizes me, clears my head, I start thinking about all the things I want to do when I am done with my walk... (which oftentimes ends up turning into a jog).

I am not saying that running or walking are the only things that will boost your energy level, but I am saying that *regular exercise* (be that yoga, Pilates, strength training, swimming, hiking, soccer, tennis, something, anything, etc.) can boost your energy level.

One of the ways that regular exercise helps your energy level is that is promotes better sleep, and usually getting a good night's sleep will help you feel more energetic the next day. It also produces that feel good endorphin, which puts you in a better mood, naturally making you feel more energetic. Exercise also typically causes you to pay more attention to what you eat and drink, so you are more inclined to make healthier choices.

Sidebar: if you are feeling sluggish, unenergetic, you may be dehydrated. In addition to regular exercise, try also making sure you are drinking enough water or other good hydration drinks (such as coconut water, Gatorade, etc.)

> *People say, "Life is not a Sprint, it's a Marathon".... I believe I now know what that means. I know that there are often obstacles that stand in our way and try to prevent us from crossing our finish line, from reaching our goals, but that's when you need to toughen up. That's where your 'don't give up' attitude comes in. Dig deep! Seek Him. Whether in a race or in any difficult situation in life. As the saying goes, "When life gets too hard to stand, kneel". Get on your knees and pray.*

Chapter 8:
'must-knows'

While the purpose of this book is not to teach you everything there is to know about running, there are a few things I would like to share, especially for any newbies.

There are so many running shoes to choose from these days, how do you know which ones are right for you? First, you need to know if you Supinate or Pronate. This is important because if you are, for example, wearing shoes designed for supinator's and you are a pronator, you could be doing more harm than good. At the very least, the shoes are not preventing your feet from the thing they are doing that needs correcting.

What is Pronation?

Pronation is the natural inward rolling motion of the foot and can sometimes overstress the body causing discomfort or injury. You should shop for Stability shoes. They will help correct your feet, so they don't turn inward as much.

What is Supination?

Supination (also known as under-pronation) is the opposite of pronation and refers to the outward roll of the foot during normal motion. You should shop for Neutral shoes. This is how my feet roll.

You can usually tell if you supinate or pronate just by looking at a pair of your shoes that you have worn a lot. If they are worn out on the outside edges, you probably supinate. If they are worn out on the inside edges you probably pronate.

You can also do a water and paper test to see. If you put down on the floor a piece of dry, blank paper, like copy paper, and get the whole bottoms of your feet wet, then step on the paper and make a foot print of each foot, you can see where your foot touches the most. Again, if you see more of a print on the outside edge of each foot, you likely supinate. If you see more of a print on the inside edge of your foot, near the arch, you probably pronate.

You can see if you have high or low (or medium) arches this way. Most running shoe websites will have a 'shoe advisor' area on their website where you can put in all the details of your foot type, where you run, how much you run, etc. and they will recommend the best shoes for you.

My 2 favorites brands are Saucony and Nike, but there are so many great brands available – it just depends on what you like, what you need and what you are willing to pay. You may want to go to a running specialty store where they can help you figure out what type of shoe you need, and they will probably be more than happy to fit you for a pair while you are there.

Another thing that is good to know about shoes: how long they last. It's a good idea to keep track how many miles you put on your running shoes, because a good pair will last for about 400 miles or so. And it's also not a bad idea to have more than one 'current' pair, so you can alternate between them. And, maybe it's just me, but I have always kind of had this rule that I only wear my running shoes while running. I never wear them as regular shoes, for casually walking around in. I don't want to waste my miles. LOL. But you could always get yourself a good pair of running shoes, since they are so comfortable and supportive, and use them specifically for walking, or wearing casually. I've done that. Did you just roll your eyes at me? Yeah, I know I'm weird, I've been told that before.

Why is pacing so important?

When you are running, you need to learn to pace yourself. A proper warm up is very important. If you start off too fast, you can burn out and the rest of your run will feel like it's going to kill you. It won't be fun.

I remember one long run, running with a woman named Mary, who was in my marathon training group. Mary naturally could run a little faster than I could. Well, we had, if I remember correctly, about a 20-mile run to do that day. I tried keeping pace with Mary, and we were enjoying the pleasant conversation, but by the time we got to about mile 9, I realized I was going too fast for me.

She went on ahead of me and I slowed down, to a little slower than my normal long run pace, and I felt so exhausted the rest of the way. It was a struggle. I never tried to do that again.

We need to figure out our own pace. The first part of your run should be a nice easy pace. And as you get warmed up, you will gradually speed up. Ideally, the second half of your run (or walk) will be faster than the first half, if you pace yourself properly. That is called a 'Negative Split'. It is a skill and takes discipline. Once you get enough practice and develop this skill well, you will be able to get up to your comfortable pace and set yourself on cruise control, as I like to call it.

I would like to note that if you are a beginner, you may be doing more of a walk/run workout, and that is totally fine! The walking can serve as your warmup. I have always encouraged people by telling them that walking is great, if you aren't able to jog/run. It's better than being a couch potato. You may eventually work up to a faster walk or longer walks. And if you can jog/run and are a beginner, it IS OK to do a walk/run. You must work your way up and build endurance. Be patient and consistent.

When I was younger and would run with my dad, he always stressed the importance of 'pacing yourself'. At that time, I didn't really get it. Now I do.

A drop about Hydration:

Our bodies are made up of about 75% water. We lose water just by the mere act of breathing (on the exhale) and through sweating and urination. So, if you think about it, it's no mystery about why it's such a big deal to stay hydrated. Some of the symptoms of dehydration are very similar to the symptoms of overhydration.

Signs of Dehydration can include: Thirst, less-frequent urination, yellow colored urine, constipation, dry cracking skin, fatigue, light-headedness, dizziness, headaches, irritability, indigestion, confusion, impaired memory, dry mouth and mucous membranes, increased heart rate and breathing.

If you are dehydrated and running (or any other form of exercise), your blood gets thicker (less water volume in it) and it's harder for your heart to pump it through, so you don't get enough oxygen.

Muscle cramping... The combination of electrolytes like sodium, calcium and potassium, along with the amount of water in your system, are responsible for keeping your muscles working properly. If you get dehydrated and that ratio is off, you can end up with painful cramping and spasming. If dehydration was serious enough, you could require a trip to an ER and some IV fluids.

Signs of Overhydration (aka: hyponatremia, or water intoxication) can include ~ fatigue, headache, confusion, nausea, vomiting, irritability, restlessness, muscle spasms, seizures, unconsciousness. These symptoms are very similar to dehydration, so how do you know which problem you might be having? I do not want to give out advice that anyone will use in place of speaking to a trained medical professional, therefore, given the seriousness of this topic, I would recommend you speak to your doctor or another medical professional, for more details on this. You can also look up information on WebMD or a similar website.

Overhydration is a pretty common thing to see in athletes doing some form of long, endurance exercise, like running a marathon. And for the runner who might be out on the race course for 4 or 5 hours, they would be the most likely candidates to drink too much water. Your body can only absorb about 8 oz. of liquid every 15 minutes, so you can use that as a guide.

An easy fix to avoid overhydration is to drink other liquids beside just water. Yes, straight water is important, but it doesn't have any electrolytes in it, so you should also drink liquids such as Powerade, Gatorade, or other Isotonic drinks which contain the electrolytes your body needs. A cup of coffee, fruit juice or a soda are acceptable additions as well.

Water intoxication (also known as overhydration or hyponatremia) is a physical condition that results from an abnormal balance of electrolytes in the body. When an overabundance of water causes an imbalance between water and electrolytes in the body, cells start to swell up. This creates a very dangerous situation as swollen cells

> *in the brain lead to intracranial pressure. As this pressure worsens, the blood flow to the brain can be interrupted, leading to dysfunction in the central nervous system, seizures, coma or even death.* Ashley Henshaw, May 7th, 2016, Symptom-Find Website.

There are also other health conditions that can contribute to overhydration, such as kidney disease, heart failure, SIADH, hormonal changes (adrenal gland and thyroid issues), age (older people generally have less sodium in their diet), various drugs, a diet low in sodium, severe vomiting or diarrhea (due to the loss of electrolytes in the blood), climate change (such as a warmer climate, leading to sweating more and in turn an electrolyte imbalance).

Post Workout Recovery:

The great thing about recovery time is that it means you just did the hard part and now you get to relax and rest up for the next time. Take a hot shower, put on some cushiony socks, or whatever makes you feel good.

When you run, your body produces the stress hormone, cortisol, because your body doesn't know if you are running for fun or running for your life! If you run out in the country, in the middle of nowhere, (in Central Texas in my case), you may actually be running for your life – away from unleashed mean dogs, angry Billy goats, (or as I like to call them, Bully goats), wild 200 lb. razorback hogs, mountain lions and what not. The exercise-reduces-stress theory kicks in *right after your run.*

Some good things to do to recover after your run, your

race or whatever workout you just did:

Hydrate, but not just with water, use an electrolyte drink of some sort – such as Powerade or Gatorade.

Be sure to eat plenty of high protein foods – because when you run, or work out, your muscles get little microscopic tears in them and protein helps repair and rebuild them. If you use gels on your long runs, (my favorite brand is Accel Gel, but there are many to choose from) you can take one of those after your run as well. The Accel Gel brand had a ratio of 4:1, carbs-protein, which is why I prefer those. Sometimes after a long run, (well usually always after a long run,) I am not hungry again for hours, so in order to take in some protein quickly, I will drink a Slim-Fast drink. There are other similar type drinks, as well, that are high in protein. Sometimes that works better than food, for me. I would just plan ahead and take a cooler with ice and have my drinks ready for after my run.

Rest, get *enough* rest, sleep, feet elevated, etc. Whatever works for you. How do you know how much is enough rest? Typically, if you wake up in the morning without an alarm clock, you probably got enough sleep.

You could also wear a pair of compression socks for the rest of the day or however long works well for you. They help encourage good circulation, which helps muscles recover. Some people like wearing them while they run, and that's OK too. I just feel too confined in them while I'm running, so I have found that they are very awesome after a hot shower and I get my feet up in the recliner!

Massages are great, and even if you don't have time for a full body massage, a foot massage is great too! If you don't have a massage therapist nearby, maybe you can go get a pedicure at a salon that does those amazing foot/calf massages as part of the treatment.

Learn how to use a foam roller (the next best thing to a massage). Keep it handy because you can use after every run or workout. I use mine after almost every run, before I even stretch. You can buy books on how to use a foam roller, but you could also "Google it" or watch a YouTube video. They are really effective at working out tight muscles/knots. Foam rolling is one of the things that helped my ITB syndrome when I was training for my first marathon.

If necessary, if you have any aches or pains that require it, you can take ibuprofen (or whatever NSAID your doctor allows) after a run, but I recommend you wait a few minutes (20-30) before taking. NSAID stands for Non-Steroidal Anti-Inflammatory Drugs. They are not recommended for long term use. They reduce the enzymes (Cox-1 and Cox-2) that play a part in producing prostaglandins, which contribute to inflammation. Sometimes, though, it's good to feel some of that discomfort so you can figure out what's causing it. It could be something in your diet, it could be overuse, not enough recovery, etc. Everyone is different and what is too much working out, too much intensity, for some people may not be too much for others. You'll need to get to know your body.

I have been dealing with RA (Rheumatoid Arthritis) for

several years now, and since that is a chronic thing, I don't want to take ibuprofen or other medications for my pain ~ since I know that what I'm dealing with is long term. Therefore, I try to focus on more natural remedies related to my diet. Turmeric, cinnamon, thyme, ground flax seed and omega-3 fatty acids are all suggested to help reduce inflammation. I use turmeric and thyme in almost all the dinners I cook. And I also put cinnamon and ground flax seed in almost everything I bake. As a matter of fact, there are a gazillion ways to use ground flax seed. Sprinkle that stuff all over like pixie dust!

Ice down any body parts that need it. Something my marathon training group used to do was, after our weekend long run, we would go soak in the ice-cold natural springs (Deep Eddy in Austin was a favorite). If you don't have anything like that available, you can always soak in an ice bath at home. And I always like to top off the ice soak with a nice relaxing bubble bath, followed by warm sweatpants (to keep the heat in). Contrast Therapy (alternating ice and heat) stimulates blood flow to your body parts, which helps in healing. The heat helps your muscles relax and it opens up your blood vessels. That allows healing nutrients and oxygen to get to the affected areas to help them heal. It also allows for cellular waste to exit the area. The ice – or cold – treatment constricts the blood vessels, causing the muscles to flex and reducing the inflammation that is causing the pain.

Chapter 9:
running bloopers and blunders

When I started training with my first marathon group, I had a lot of firsts. We were doing long runs longer than I had ever done. I was always learning something new. One Saturday, I wasn't sure how long we'd be out on the trail, I just knew it was going to be a few hours. So, just to make sure I didn't 'run' into any embarrassing trouble, *I took an extra tampon with me on the run. I stuck it down in my sports bra between my boobs, until I would need it later.* I didn't think about all the sweat that would be passing through there…So let me tell ya', it sure did a good job at soaking up all the sweat!

Another funny thing I learned while out on a 10-mile run is that if you are going to be running in the rain, don't wear a lot of deodorant or hairspray or body lotion, etc. What had happened was… I had all of the above on and part way through our run it started raining. After a good amount of time had passed of sweating a lot and getting rained on, I happened to look down for whatever reason and I noticed I was foaming at the crotch. I said to my coach, "I think I have come down with crotch rabies. I'm foaming." He just laughed and explained how that happens.

There is a race in Austin every year called the Chuy's 5K. People dress up in costumes, if they so please, and it can be very entertaining to see them all. But this one race, I had already finished and was just hanging out near the finish line cheering for other runners and I saw this couple come through with interesting tops on. They had gotten my attention, so I had to take a closer look at what it was. Oh, be-jeepers!!! They were almost totally naked except for a thong on her and a bikini bottom on him! And the woman (who was up there in years and not quite as perky as her 20-something year old counterparts) had drawn a picture of a droopy ear dog face (or something to that effect) on her upper half. All I could do was just think "OMG" and try really hard to get the image out of my head. But some things you just can't 'un-see'.

Here's a disgusting one: one time I was running the Jingle Bell 5K and it was a night race right around Christmas time, so it was cold. And with cold weather comes running noses, and that means runners spitting 'honkers' out all over the road. Gross! IT was everywhere, you couldn't take a step without coming into contact with it – and let me just say, it's slippery! Barf city! Excuse me for a moment….

While we are on the subject of spit… once during a 20-mile race (being used as a training long run) it happened to be a pretty cold and windy day in Texas, in January. I had settled into a pace that was about the same as this guy in a blue sweatshirt, so we were side by side for quite a while. Unfortunately, for me, I had dropped back in behind him for a minute (using him as a windbreaker) and he seemed to be a little mucousy. How do I know that, you asked? Because he started spitting his 'honkers' and one of them landed on me! Oh my gosh! Talk about Rude! And super disgusting! Gah!

I can remember another time, different year, this same 20-mile run, in Round Rock, TX it was only supposed to be about 19 degrees when we started and maybe get into the 30's for the high that day. I dressed in layers, like you should, so that as I warmed up I could shed some layers if I needed to. One of the mistakes I made was wearing one of those knit head wraps around my neck to keep it warm. By the end of the 20 miles I had a 3" wide hickie looking mark all the way around my neck from the chaffing! And do you know, chaffing stings really bad when water touches it… IE: your shower after your run.

Reasons People Run:

1) He met a pretty girl at Disney and she is a runner, so he 'became' a runner.
2) Because the wine store closes in 20 minutes and I have to get there in time. (Julie Gladstone)
3) Running is my therapy. (Christy Egan)
4) It's like meditation, and it makes me feel better mentally. (Samantha Scarborough)
5) I run because when I'm running I am free. (Ron, 5minproject)
6) Because it's free, you don't have to pay a membership fee and you can do it almost anywhere. Anonymous contributor.
7) I run for the mental clarity and toughness it offers. At a certain point you need one to get the other.

(Arend Pryor)
8) So people can stand being around me, LOL! Goo day run, bad days run harder! (Elicia Bagnardi)
9) Because someone's chasing me. (Karen Kemp)
10) I run to relieve stress, to think through my problems, and to connect with God. Running can be very spiritual for me sometimes. (jessieandtex)

Words of inspiration:

Tommy's First Marathon Experience: "If I could give someone advice on running a marathon, it would be "Don't Do It!" Just Kidding!! It would be to take it seriously and be sure to train and eat properly. It never hurts to have someone who's done a marathon to talk to for tips and advice. I had my sister Angie for that. She helped me out a lot. Especially about food and drinks that speed up recovery after long training runs. And for Encouragement. There were a few times that I questioned why I'd want to punish my body the way running 26.2 miles does. But it's one of the most gratifying things ever when you cross the finish line. We both ran and finished the 2009 Country Music Marathon. It was special because our father, who was quite a runner in his day, was there to watch us both cross the finish line. He unexpectedly passed away later in that same year. It was really cool to share the experience with Dad and Angie. He was real proud of us." ~ Tommy Mills, Jr.

Parting words of encouragement (and humor):

Some parting words I would like to share with you, as we are finishing this race and walking our cool down.

Like I said before in the introduction, *Running Defines Me*. It's who I am. I would be lost if I couldn't run. And I feel like it's important to share with you that I believe the only reason I'm still running, *and loving it*, after 40 something years, is because I don't do it to be better than **anybody** else. I don't run races to come in first place. When I run, it's all about doing better than "I" did the day before, the week before, the last race PR, and so on. I compete against myself. Against the part of my brain that says, "I'm too tired, I have no energy, I can't do this" and the part of me that says "You were born to run, you have what it takes, you are a winner, push yourself, feel the burn, don't quit, and no matter what…. Never Ever Give Up".

The days that I get suited up for a run and just don't feel like it, no energy, no enthusiasm, or what have you, those are the days I end up having my best runs. I think it ends up being a reward for just doing it, even when I didn't feel like it that day.

Something else I feel is important to note, with my love of running, is that I am not ever running *away from* anything. Metaphorically speaking. As a matter of fact, I think that my marathoning experiences have taught me how to stand and fight for it, to stick with it when it's hard, to never give up or give in and to know it will be worth it in the end. The "it" in all of this is whatever you are facing in life that is hard or challenging. Whatever it is that makes you want to quit or give up. Your marriage, your job, your relationships with your children or others, your financial situation, whatever the case may be.

There have been times in my life when I gave up too easy and walked away, on important life matters, where I should have stayed and fought hard and not been a quitter. I have since then, in my marathoning years, learned better. I pray that for you and myself, we can be strong, give it our all and never give up. No matter what comes our way.

The only things I would ever tell you to *run away from* are growling dogs, angry goats and prowling mountain lions, and whatever else goes chasing you in your imagination!

Now get out there and get going! Make me proud!

Run for Your Life!!   i. am. runner.

BOOK REVIEWS:

"Run for Your Life" by Angie Mills is an inspiring collection of stories about running, the love of running, and the meaning of running. Runners looking for a boost to kick-start a running routine, as well as veteran marathoners who share Angie's passion for running, will find humor, motivation, and affirmation in the pages.

Paul Carmona.

A lawyer by trade, Paul Carmona has spent his "spare time" coaching runners since 2004. What started in Austin, Texas, as coaching beginners on the basics of running has grown into a worldwide following of runners. "Coach Paul" now trains hundreds of runners across the United States, and some as far away as the United Kingdom and South America, through online coaching with Revel Online Coaching, Brooksee Online Coaching, and Twenty-Six Two Marathon Club.

Paul has run every day since February 2, 2013, and has completed 59 marathons as of May 2018, a 100-mile ultramarathon, one Ironman Triathlon, and dozens of half-marathons and triathlons over the years. An 8-time finisher of The Boston Marathon, he specializes in helping runners train to qualify for Boston.

Paul still coaches the First-Time Marathoner group in Austin, Texas, which is where he got his start coaching with Angie Mills and the other women who trained for San Diego Rock 'N' Roll in 2005. And he still coaches that group for free.

"I am so impressed with Angie's Book, "Run for Your Life". She eloquently articulates the meaning of life and the clarity and depth running has brought to her. This book will help many understand why so many runners continue the lifestyle. I hope this becomes a standard issue from individuals who are helping others get into running and how life changing it can be."

Paul Carrozza

Paul Carrozza is a business owner who is passionate and commitment to promoting health and fitness in the community and around the nation.

An accomplished All-American athlete and a seasoned coach, Paul is committed to developing quality programs and events that contribute to the economic growth in the community and help increase the quality of life in the greater Austin area.

He is a Husband, father of three and an avid promoter of family fitness and educational programs. A Member of President Bush's Council of Fitness and Sports, Co-Chair of Governor Perry's Advisory Council on Fitness for the State of Texas, Chair of the Mayor of Austin Council on Fitness, Chair of the Small Business Division of the Austin Chamber of Commerce, Chairman of the Board of Carrozza Foundation, Austin Marathon Foundation, Shoes for Austin. He is also the Founder and Producer, Willie Nelson's 10K for Farm Aid, Founder and Producer of RunTex Marathon Kids, Founder and Producer of Motorola/Freescale/Austin Marathon and Founder of RunTex Events.

Made in the USA
Columbia, SC
21 September 2021